Monologue Dogs

Monologue Dogs
Méira Cook

Brick Books

Library and Archives Canada Cataloguing in Publication

Cook, Méira, 1964–, author
    Monologue dogs / Méira Cook.

Poems.
Issued in print and electronic formats.
ISBN 978-1-77131-357-5 (pbk.).—ISBN 978-1-77131-359-9 (pdf).—
ISBN 978-1-77131-358-2 (epub)

    I. Title.

PS8555.O567M65 2015   C811'.54   C2014-907983-4
                                               C2014-907984-2

We acknowledge the Canada Council for the Arts, the Government of Canada through the Canada Book Fund, and the Ontario Arts Council for their support of our publishing program.

The author photo was taken by Robyn Shapiro.
The book is set in Sabon.
Cover image by Natalie Waldburger.
Design and layout by Marijke Friesen.
Printed and bound by Sunville Printco Inc.

Brick Books
431 Boler Road, Box 20081
London, Ontario N6K 4G6

www.brickbooks.ca

for my Stereo Boys

((for Misha and Shai))

CONTENTS

Bone Shop / 1

The Hunger Artists / 27

Mongrel Heart / 43

Crooked / 67

Bone Shop

THE DEVIL'S ADVOCATE

My lords and ladies, gentlemen of the jury—
when you hear hoofbeats, assume horses, not zebras.
This is true in almost all parts of the world
except the African savannah, where it is safer
to assume zebras. Also eland, giraffes, herds
of this and that. In India, assume cows; in Spain,
bulls, matadors with their sun-blurred hooves.
In Tuscany, angels; in Kingdom Come, horses again,
pale quartets of Wish You Were Here.

My client sends his regrets. He is busy
falling through blank verse for all eternity, while a mere afternoon
passes its shadow over us. The sun moves from one window
of the courthouse to the next, and then it's tea time.
One sugar or two? Perhaps a bun. Stretch
and yawn and back we go. I submit
for your perusal Exhibit A.
This is a map of the world, of God, and of everything.
Above is heaven, below is hell—

the future is to the right, the past to the left.
My client, in his plea for mercy, wishes me to recall
his salient points. His sense of humour, direction, and yes, style,
his tendency to violent foreshortenings, and that finding
himself irredeemably zebra, he hoofed the streets
of his brawling, captious nature, kicking
up dust and all the limping platitudes
of this earth, our home. They tell you dreams
don't come true. But they never tell you how.

HERE AM I

My people have sixteen words by which to avoid
the name of God. I called on all of them.
Moriah was the mountain, Isaac my son—
a knife, a ram, a fire, a father. The knife began, it rang
suns like bright coins on its blade, drew blood from my gaze
while a drunken ram tossed us about on the horns
of its shabby implausible dilemma.

Here's a riddle: what is upright
as an index finger yet can be folded in half
like a stone tablet? Men cut their fingers on its pages
but children tear out and devour the middle.
A book, a loaf? The Law
is only a knife cutting the world into before
and after. The rocks were full of eyes

and the desert emptied its pockets of us,
we fell hard against the sand. The iguana-eyed rocks
of Genesis, of Are We There Yet?
For years the neighbours whispered
about fathers and sons, gods and knives, decisions
illogical as that neon sun. For years
until I died. And even afterwards.

THE FLY-AWAY GIRL

Only thing to cut the heat is a lemon, thick and sour.
The garden jumps backwards and forwards
between the legs of cicadas and grasshoppers.
Flying home at the first sign of grievance
the ladybugs are always too late,

and their children burn with a long sin.
Someone has left that sun-bulb on again,
all those electric rays jerking through
the wild blue jump.
Open a wing blade, bird hum. Fly away, sky.

Summer breaks open in the sun.
Ants carry away the crumbs. Glossy black
sentences crawl from the Book of Summer
lying beneath the trees. Here is the lemon tree
and here is my mouth.

Sour enough to take the edge off memory, honey.

THE COME-BACK KID

From far away the garden is empty
as beckoning. *Hello again,*
hello, it's me. It's only me.
Here is the garden (empty)
and here is my mouth (open).

Open my mouth and all the birds
of late summer fly out,
list on telephone lines, listening.
Oh clock-birds! Break with time,
escape the mechanical

clockwork of winter.
Far away the garden is empty, the hasty
distracted ghosts long gone. Men deal cards
in the dust. A woman shuffles her hands, a mother
calls in the dusk. *Come in, girl, get a move on.*

Meaning *here*, meaning *hurry*, meaning *home*.

CRACKED

Young Eve

Summer's head of cabbage, each next
breath, the garter snakes oozing from the undergrowth,
fat ripples of black and gold. Some loose

green fuse tripped our intention.
I drove north along the highway with my boyfriend
in his daddy's pickup, looking for a place to park.

The day had a crack down the middle
was one way of looking at it.
Then I opened my shirt and unhitched my bra,

more for the relief of air than his distraction
although I achieved both.
Before was the garden, after the burn of day

down to the wick, the scuffle and cut,
his mouth stubbed out against my own.
And where did you hear we were naked

is what I want to know? Unzip unzip—
my jeans round my ankles, his open at the waist.
Blames me for what happened next, wants to snap

my thighs for a wishbone. As if there were wishes
(there are none). As if he could extinguish
himself in me.

Her Boyfriend

Her mouth a wound, rubbing salt.
Love was not a word we would have used.
Begin again. Everything was dying,

the sky ticked in spasms above us.
Then the tomatoes began muttering
blood and *wince* and *cut*. All synonyms

for love. For love I cut
my losses, each loss
eased her reckless burn.

Some cold hard seed
pushing hunger out of the earth.
A craving for salt or sufficiency

or vegetable lust. An accidental,
misshapen thing. Let me begin
again. What about free will?

What about the angels, crunching their obedient
apples and trimming their beards?
The garden was the beginning. Where she first

coincided with herself. She was my north,
my south, my worst, my best. Her thin bones
my compass, her languor my rest.

Any Old Snake

He suffered in the rind of summer.
Hot winds cracked the surface of days, and birds
fell from the sky, their eyeholes trailing smoke.

Children spun like scarecrows in empty fields,
the river rattled its broken spine in the dust,
and the dead swelled up and blew as we watched.

That's life, she said. *You'll find sympathy
in the dictionary between shit and syphilis.*
She was sixteen and seeding like dandelion,

blown on the wind, selving. Somewhere
in the night a train whistled through town,
a screen door banged open, shut.

We needed a garden or the idea of a garden,
an annihilating, green-shaped thought
to cast some shade.

IACHIMO

> *On her left breast*
> *A mole cinque-spotted: like the crimson drops*
> *I' the bottom of a cowslip . . .*
> — Shakespeare, *Cymbeline* II, ii.

Meanwhile, Imogen prepares a kiss
strung like a jewel between words:
ruby-virtue, uh huh and *pearl-queasy, darlin'*.
This kiss is never delivered, but ripens
on her lips, yields
a drop of blood a day.

The kiss against which all waiting
grows anemic. In her chamber Imogen slams
flies between the covers of her novel.
Her first mistake, a woman
wearies of the book
fattening in her hands and falls

asleep. The moon and I
enter stage left. One halves itself,
the other doubles, thumbing through her punctual,
unpunctuated skin. While all the sticky girls
dream of honey and hooves, of lovers
consigned to dust, golden boys tarnishing as they breathe.

When her husband arrives on the scene,
late by name and nature,
I turn back the covers of his incredulity.
There! Do you see it, you fool?
How every dog can have his bone of her!
Poor, tardy Posthumus—and Imogen,

Imogen dying, Imogen dead, Imogen fallen
to jigsaw in his head. But when he tries
to put her together again
there is a piece, cinque-spotted,
that doesn't quite fit,
no matter where he moves it.

THE *GAMÍADAS* OF VASCO DA GAMA: AN EPIC

What kind of explorer believes there is no ocean
because all he can see is land?
There was a sneeze in the world that would not be sneezed,
a nasal irritation blocking the sinus passages
of old Europe.
So we sailed to the New World, un-
Edened, dragging
the creaking wooden future behind us.

In your own good time, said my King, clasping himself
about the equator.
There wasn't a moment to lose, though winter
and the wind fretted the edge of the continent
like a bit of cheap cloth. But my Queen was dreaming
of the sun shining through her cat's ears.
Silk! she murmured, *Silk!* By which she meant *India*
and *begone* and *hurry up* and *don't go*.

My Catarina, my wife, my stone in the shoe, my life!
I was leaving on a journey, a voyage, a discovery. I was
resolved to halve the world's surface and double its bounty,
resigned to the death of compatriots, enemies, comrades, crew.
My own when it came would be glorious, I knew,
cast in bronze, hoisted in every city from Lisbon to Calcutta.
Don't forget your woolens dear, she kissed me on the brow,
my Lady of the Sorrows, my figure on the prow.

Love is the longitude that runs through the middle of the world,
dividing as the spine the body, all enterprise.
She was my East my East my East my East—
but I returned each time to claim her as an undiscovered country.
Six sons, a daughter, and only one of dubious paternity,
and I am likely mistaken—everyone said so. Although,
only one white crow is required to disprove our smug taxonomies.
How elegant! All crows being black; all wives treacherous.

We come now to the Pilgrim Ship Incident, history rustling
its pages, the odour of dust
on old stories. *Why delay?* asks my Queen, sand sifting
from her navel. I died long ago in the city of Cochin
but my body returned to Portugal in a gold casket.
Tell me about the women, she says, *who brought you their gold
and their babies. What weighs more, a pound of gold
or a pound of baby?*

That year the smoke of pilgrim grease
hung a meat-flag above the burning ship
for days. Each day grabbed night by the shoulders and turned
with the sun's tight quarter-turn. I was the centre of the world
and our world the centre of the universe, though we'd set out to prove
the opposite. First the pilgrims burned for God
and then they burned for me, and the priest with donkey's ears
sewn into his head, by my command, ran braying into eternity.

How does a man survive his death? In his wife's ambiguities,
his mistress's certainty? In his children's regard
or lack of it? Those born on this side of the blanket, the others
the other. I had a story to tell, a bolt of silk to unroll
along a reputation worn slippery with ill use.
Somewhere there is a church, an opera, a minor port city.
Three football clubs in the colonies bear my name,
a mascot, a mall and, on dark nights, the moon.

Did I say moon? Honour, dishonesty, the body's bright rot,
are candles to light up the dead. But I have nothing
save the currency of my good name rubbed dull as pennies
on a dead man's eyes. It wasn't the full moon or the half.
Nor even the quarter moon or the merest scribble of light
in the eastern sky like the wake of a ship writing
lost, lost on the water. You'll know by now it was a crater
they named for me. A hole, an emptiness.

Vasco da Gama, old man in the moon, old
rock-faced, wall-eyed Who D'ya Think You Are?
All my life I've tried to catch memory as it flew by
like winged fish evading that splendid trawl of Forgetfulness
and Again. The fishermen pack their boats.
All they've caught is the moon, too small to eat.
They toss it back. They know that moons are treacherous
and heroes are frail and cynicism is the dearest illusion of all.

YOUNG EVE, ALL GROWN UP

The Angel Gabriel comes to me, all bone and leather
held together by ego and a gubernatorial pose.
It wasn't night, I wasn't dreaming.

You're looking well, young Eve, he says, ignoring
the scaffolding that rivets the past in place: breath,
scales, subtlety, old grudges, old ribs, an ancient

electric sword flashing in the dark. No You Don't/Don't You Dare.
And always the same kids squabbling over their daddy's
share—the meagre, worm-digested earth

of his love. Somewhere my old man waits for me,
his eyes blown like dandelion clocks
past the hour of sobriety.

I was midrib to his leaf until a tree sprang up between us
and then a forest and then a Library of Imaginary Books
about trees, forests, deciduous thoughts.

Too much! All the green-blooded world
staunched between the covers of paperback novels
thickened by the fall

into cooling baths and the drying out
on late-night radiators.
The Angel turns out his pockets

and holds up his hands. He is searching
for the garden we lost once
and every day since.

Verde que te quiero verde, he whispers in my ear.
Green, how much I want you green.
Green wind. Green branches.

I look everywhere, scattering sins
like pomegranate seeds. Breaking the law
with my bare hands.

Disobedience is the way back: a lie, a lapse, a bite
of something plucked
not fallen.

The Angel Gabriel straightens his arthritic wings
and shuffles off in his crushed-heel slippers
and his scuffed ideals,

while around us in the desert
some damn memory wavers and grows steady,
blooms, shimmers, and dies again,

which is to say *green*. Green I want you,
old fracture, old friend. Green branches on the green wind,
green marrow whistling through pale green bone,

and in the Library of Imaginary Books
poems ripen, wet and lush,
as time-lapse fruit inside their husks.

EASING THE SPRING

My Mother's Daughter

My mother waits with me in the warning flare
of dawn, where the subway gapes
like a hungry mouth, rattling cars, rattling teeth.
And tries to warm me at the tips of her blue
fingers, winter's thinnest fire.
And tries to feed me, scratching meat off a bone
from the Greek takeaway on Third.
And wears away my face as she does every year

around this time, by the looking—and I hers.
We are waiting for him and his gold-edged invitation.
For which read *come!* And *hurry, girl!*
For which read *guilt!* Bad Translations
is a game he plays on winter nights when the dead
open all their eyes in the dark, a peacock's tail,
which is not to say they have died in vain.
Around us ghosts lope into the future, sway

their gamey bellies this way and that, as if appetite
is an iron clapper. *Sonnez la cloche! Sonnez la cloche!*
They do not walk backwards or behind us or into the past.
These days the dead travel swiftly, salt on their tails,
leading their half-shell lives in double time. My mother
devotes herself to virtuous translations: for rivers,
stone into silt; for spiders, saliva into silk. For mothers,
Nothing To Be Done into hurry, into spilt, into milk.

Morning stumbles about on broken ankles,
calling for light. In the subway, Rapid Transit
offers half-price deals: Let the Dead
Carry Their Dead and You Won't Look Back With Us.
High heels along the rails, the rats swerving their tails,
the metallic fall of my mother's thoughts all
clatter. But still he does not come, though we twitch
with shame, iron filings at the mention of his name.

Hush now, she comforts me, but the season has turned
on its fulcrum, the green hinge of the year latched shut.
Soon her daughter will be gone, the past and the future
gnashing their teeth, baring themselves
in an endless, weary grin.
My mother stuffs packets of food in my pockets,
but the end of my hunger is only the beginning
of hers.

Soon he will step into the burning street
and snap his fingers,
summoning the sun to glide off his gilded nails.
All ten nails, all ten suns.
And my mother blooms like the stars you see
when you ram into a tree, a kiss,
old bony inevitability. My mother flowers, a rose
in the eye from the fist of someone who loves you.

Her Mother

Wherever she's gone I can be summoned by the pull
of memory's thick gold tassel
from the kitchen where I hunker all winter, plotting
my small kitchen revenges,
to the top of the house where my children wander
wringing their hands and muttering about favouritism.
Does one love a child more because she is lost
and found, borrowed and lent, saved and spent?

Guilt! I roar. I am the match put to the pilot light
of the old gas cooker. A steady flame but the heat
is uneager. *Oh Demeter, I saw your daughter,
last night. She's turning black, poor thing.*
Then something about the cheap fruit they sell
at the Market. Windfall and sour and swollen
with seed. Guilt, then the cheap fruit.
Sometimes dried, sometimes forced, bruised,

overused as needless advice.
*Don't eat the fruit, little children, or the seeds
of the fruit, or drink the juice.*
The children push out their lips,
hard rub of teeth beneath, and the limits
of my temper past all reaching, teaching
that not everything lost may be recovered.
Oh, my daughter! My laughter, my wild

wild honey of the heart. Far below
the subway tracks and the rats' feet and the bodies
flinging themselves between the *thunka thunka
thunk* of wheel against steel-jawed longing,
below igneous and the knock of teeth
against rock and all the dead darlings
running through the dark, rattling their bones
and crying, *Time's up! Time's up!*

Rampant on a field of white linen,
this man, this god, this plan.
Hello, knife! Good Morning, blade that cuts
the summer from the fall, the Fall
from what comes after pride, before gravity, beyond the parade
of mourning. That cuts the shade from the tree, the mother
from Persephone. And the cheap pomegranates
they sell at the Market? Windfall! Windfall!

It's getting late, light flashes off the windows
of buildings and streetcars. The year runs straight
off its tracks.
Soon he'll step into the burning street, my daughter will sway
and falter on her feet. *Listen for the bees,* she will say.
But who knows if they'll come this year, the thrum,
the stir of half-past thaw, an open door
easing the spring?

The Hunger Artists

Once upon a time a mother ...

I could say not hard or not very often
or his pain was worse than mine.
I could say I deserved it,
or I don't remember, not much,
or hunger is a flame blued through to salt.

First the rats come out of the fields
and into the city,
like one great rat with a million mouths
and each mouth with a thousand teeth
and the will to grind our lives exceedingly small.

Then hunger enters without knocking,
as if he's lived here forever.
He lays a place at the table and draws up a chair.
*Good evening, good evening. Pass the butter, do.
My goodness, this porridge is thin!*

The more he eats the leaner he becomes.
A skeleton, a piece of gristle, a singing bone.
The brats climb into my belly
and begin to gnaw their way out again,
cracking me like an egg,

not in half but in pieces.
I have put all my yolks in one basket,
now I can't sleep for the sound
of lapping in the dark.
In the morning, a cough of eggshell

on the sheets and the brats lolling
with their blue Persian tongues.
My darlings, my parasites!
One day their father returns
from the empty fields and the empty seas

and the sky where nothing grows.
Hunger, my lover, sits at the head of the table,
sharpening his knives and his teeth,
while the brats crawl
from their mother's eyes.

Little maggoty things, little grubs that feed
on the truculent gaze.
I could say not hard.
Not very hard at all. I could say
pain is a proof in the Theorem of Love,

or something less complicated to do
with the bruise and the sweetness
of the after-fruit.
I thought God would hear.
I knew the neighbours wouldn't.

Little children, little children!

GRETEL

The days ring with frost, the days
arranged like a table setting of thin-stemmed
wine glasses, each one filled to a different level.
We run up and down the length of days,
ringing at their rims till they sing.

HANSEL

Street lights hum the darkness along
the long nursery highway.
Then the geese fly away, folding the sky
into arrows and paper airplanes and winter. Once
there was method in my madness. Now, only method.

GRETEL

My mother's breath smells of acetone.
It peels the paint off us, and yes it chills to the bone,
as cold as a lost key
left in a parked car, dead of winter.
Get into the car, little children.

HANSEL

In the middle of the night. A forest sprang up.
Get into the car, says my mother. The forest
changes gears, grating.
The forest makes a sound like the whir
of windup bears in old stories.

GRETEL

Inside the books it is snowing, the snow
falls all night and in the morning
our childhood is over. A turned page.
The forest turns over
like a snow globe and hangs there.

HANSEL

Suddenly the car drops down on all fours
and will go no farther. *Arrival is neither here
nor there*, Mother says, searching for her key.
But her key is in the last lost pocket of the world's
overcoat and tonight—tonight the forest is ajar.

GRETEL

Here is a list of Interesting Things to Salt:
A bucket of snails (for foam).
The dying flames of a fire (for blue).
An open wound (for pain).
The ground, Mother, after you.

HANSEL

Some rules for Getting Out Alive:
Don't play tug-of-war with a tree.
Don't bet against the house, the house
always wins in the end. And never lick
a gingerbread house on a cold morning.

GRETEL

The birds eat the salt and sicken.
The birds are preserved from the inside out,
learn their lesson and never look back.
Meanwhile, in another part of the forest, there is a cage,
an appetite, a hunger. Brought together in perfect accord.

HANSEL

Oh, my sister, my chimera! You are my real-true, long-legged
thing. My psychosomatic joy, my gone-again pain, my nerves
strummed to sinew. Nobody believes you
like I do though I rub salt, *cum grano salis*,
on all your short cuts home.

GRETEL

Even the storks know you can't go home again
or even once. They have lost all sense of decorum,
now they teeter about on stilts, setting their toy fires
in all the wrong chimneys. Oh, my brother, my beloved
Terror—sing, sing your gold-skinned psalms.

HANSEL

This is how the story ends. There is no witch,
no oven, no wild mother stalking her hunger
through the forest. No sister tossing the bones,
tithing her little store of jealousy and grief.
Hunger fights Appetite to the death.

GRETEL

My brother is locked in the old iron forest.
All night he calls for me to bring my keys.
This is how the story ends. I carry him
on my back, in my heart.
He enters my bloodstream, a virus raging.

HANSEL

On quiet afternoons, half-dreaming
in the thick grass, I watch my sister
running barefoot through the high blue fields.
She is searching for me or for what has become of me,
the breakup, the runoff, the bloom.

But their father comes for them...

Jacob Grimm, tell me if you know
how to douse the eye's light?
I see a mother lead her children, and mine,
into a darkness scored with points of light
like the missing nails that once held

The House of Pain in place.
It is an old house but a good one;
it has served, like us, its time.
Now all the clocks are wringing their hands
and turning their faces to the walls.

Jacob Grimm, the dark arches its back
inside the box of the riddle-cat.
The cat plays all the angles,
the angle of possum, the angle of perception.
But how do we know if the cat

is alive, if the cat is alight
or a liar? And how do the children survive
their mother's darkness?
                        Jacob Grimm, tell me
if you know, is that the rot

of catgut or the rank breath of a forest
digesting the dainty bones?
The House of Pain was a house for listening
to the rain when it fell. I miss the rain, it had
a dying fall.

The darkness, the damned, the light
from dead stars fall but not like the rain
on the tin roof of the House of Pain
where we lived in the years called Whileaway
because they did not last forever.

I am an old man, Jacob Grimm, in a dry month,
and all the stories are burning
from the tops of their heads,
set alight by children afraid of the dark.
Running forever into the forever-vanishing.

And they all lived, says Jacob Grimm . . .

Here's how it begins. My sister Lotte
knows the stories.
My brother Wilhelm writes them down.
Our mother yanks open the forest
and throws us all inside.

The birds have eaten the bread crumbs,
cries Lotte. And the cats have eaten
the birds. (*The wolves the cats*, says Wilhelm,
the axe the wolves.) In the end,
not even the Angel of Death can stomach

such hunger. Here's how it goes. The stories
circle us and begin to wail.
We are just dreams, they say. *If you die
we will never be born.* One by one, the stories
step forward and offer their names.

Han-sel, says one. *Gre-tel*, says another.
*Ah, that is butter. Ah, that is honey
on warm bread*, sighs Lotte, licking her fingers,
and Wilhelm is already straddling the one
called Rumpelstiltskin. Around us,

the stories kneel down on all fours.
The hunger to be borne is an animal
offering its haunch for the mad dash
through the jaws of *enough enough
enough*. Here's how it begins

again. My brother, my sister, look back
at me with keyhole looks. Already
they're growing smaller, red helium
memories tied with string. Or how
time flows both ways

when the river thaws. Spring is still
a palindrome here in the Hanau valley.
Dear Lotte, Dear Wilhelm, once upon a time
every story was the story
of our mother's starvation. The wild

wild hunger that stalked her as she followed
her stiff white breath into the forest,
throwing us, like grains of salt, over her shoulder.
For luck, for love. For ever,
if only we'd known what ever was for.

Mongrel Heart

THE TALKING CURE

Those were the days when women
in pale frocks and powdered shoulders
were moths flaring against the dying
light of summer evenings.

Sun through leaves turned lawn
to torn lace. Bee-static in the fizzing grass
and the *pock* of leather against willow, though
no one's played cricket here for years.

The sound of Might Have Been in the country
of Good Enough, Pal. The sound
of parallel lines converging on our bastard past.
When the last of the colonists left, rounding

the gravel sweep and waving
their languid hands, night bloomed
poison fruit on the branches
of oleander and hemlock. We fell sick,

each one for a different reason.
One ate too many melons
from a jar marked *melancholy*, one
got lost in the middle of her dark wood.

One was cut bloody as mown lawn,
one began to seep ideas, the fluid running
to infection within days.
One contracted a rare strain of happiness

which proved fatal, the only death.
One aimed herself straight at God,
one couldn't extinguish the burning
filaments of her eyes.

One fell like a feather, one fell like a stone
and for all time.
One had to keep walking
to wear out her pain, one

filled up every morning with rage
like blood in a ballet dancer's shoes.
One cut herself down to size
on the blade of a life. And one

waved at the sea but the sea
waved goodbye. The sun
spun in the sky, a coin,
lost and won too many times

in a game called Empire.
Or a coin balanced on the rails
to be flattened
by some new-fangled invention,

a locomotive or a subconscious.
And here it comes ... *thunka thunka
thunka*: the new century,
panting down the tracks towards us.

LEAR IN AFRICA

Her Daddy

In the heat of the day the pariah dogs sleep
in their revolving shadows.
Their loose skin, twitching dreams.
The earth spins, snatching
all they own or ever will,
a minute's shade. Even cloud-scrape
over stubble can't wake them.
When the starvelings tie their tails together
and set them alight they sleep on,
burning up for peace in this dark place.

Did I say for peace—I meant for love.

His Best Girl

Truth is a dog kennelled in the dark,
darkest place of the heart. Truth
rattles in the night with heavy slow links,
this way and that, all night.
In the morning a cuff of bright red
jointing the bone.
Come my darling, my mongrel, my father,
we are what's left, you and I.
And the stink of ripeness from over a wall.
And love, the pebbledash graininess of

some humdrum steadfast love.

Her Daddy

They bore me away on my funeral bier,
wind-whipped my blood, unstrung
my bones. No longer king, I was a dog
amongst dogs. The dogs in this country
pant in the dust, scorn the flies
that jewel their eyes, scorn the fires
crackling out of the earth. Everything
is the king of something. They are kings
of the tapeworm winding its way
through the gut.

Many years, worms, hungers.

His Best Girl

They carried you away, your throat open
to the stars. Monstrous
and stylish at last in your dark
red scarf. Somewhere a dog howled
in the night. Not a dog in a legend
or tapestry or ballad. But a real-true stink dog,
it must have been, the only kind
that couldn't rouse you.
Then packs of them fell into step,
all the three-legged, one-eyed creatures

of this mongrel century, howling.

Daddy

I came back for you, Cordiality.
One of the punctual dead who return, wringing
their hands to rag. From far above I saw
an old man, a deposed king, a corpse
on a stretcher.
Quite the driest month of the year, the hill
dragging a road away on its back.
Fires flashed from thin air, wheeling
great hoops of flame towards us.
But when you opened your dead eyes, the pinwheels

of love and madness whirled together.

Girl

What is a dog in this country? What
is a daughter? Four-legged, panting.
We follow our masters about, pressing our snouts
into their self-regard. When trapped we will gnaw
our hearts to the bone.
My salt-love could not season or preserve,
it was a deficient thing, a flea, a tick,
a pulse of blood.
And when I died no honey bubbled
from the earth in springs. No rooster,

violently red and triple-crowned, crowed.

FIVE ACT ISCARIOT

Act I

Come walk with me a while beneath the trees,
Gethsemane is cool tonight, the moon
is full, a coin tossed in a game of chance.
And metal as the metal leaves that strike
small gleams against the dark, the sullen oil
rag of dreams. Near and far, stars fall and burn,
dead things they are, but full of light—I know
them well. All night wind gutters until dawn,
gone, foregone. And in the morning some still
small voice speaks out: *For all the rest it's true*

that any dog can have its bone of you.

Act II

What sound is that? What liniment stink? What
fallen creature shakes itself to tatters
on the branch. Crow is not a sound, crow is
the hunger towards ripeness, rot. The sweet
dead heat. Crow is the kiss before the fall.
Dawn whips about on the end of night's rope.
Somewhere there is a rope waiting for me
to grab hope of. I meant nothing by *kiss*.
Too late, too late, the garden fades beneath
rumours of leaf, light, grief—and you and I

forever searching and forever lost.

Act III

Another crow? That's two, you say, one more
to go. I know nothing of *crow*, my Lord.
The trees are searching for the moon; the moon,
like us, is lost. We are gamblers, gambling
to lose. Come close now, take my cloak, I want
to whisper in your ear, Lord, to tell you
that love is not meek, a cheek-turning hymn.
Love is the choral hum of flies, love lays
its eggs in the body and the body
lights up, hums and hurts in the dark. No dog

will touch you. *Noli me tangere!* Don't come

Act IV

so close. Years teetering at the margins
of documentary, love neither mild
nor kind vented up through my ribs; that caught
bird, my heart. Well, what do you know of love?
It is rivers bursting into flame, seeds
boiling in the earth. It is brokenness—
Jacob wrestling the angels out of joint,
and lovers, star-throated, their skin coming
off like moth dust, dying, dying. So, love.
And, yes, I heard it too. The third, the last.

Each object spins on its own thrown shadow—

Act V

then dawn, the clatter of metallic light
from the east, all hospitality fled.
And love. How it is drawn against the flesh
or withdrawn. How it is given, gotten,
and forgotten. Quick! Catch the tarnished moon,
one last lucky coin to hold in your palm
as the rising dawn heaves up and splinters
on some stretched wooden stagecraft of the mind.
And in that light a simple thing—not kind,
not mild, but blank-eyed, rough, with sweat-streaked brow—

passes in shadow over I and Thou.

THE ALMOST-BOY

Liar! yelled God. But Geppetto was the kind of father
who liked to knock things into place. First
was a grin on his terrible face (he held it there
with nails, he held it there with resolution).
The second was Mr. Bones, that loose-

hinged, cartilage-jawed whatsit.
Rubbing him raw from inside his loose death.
(He took out his ball-peen Forever and hammered out
a boy.) Which was also the third thing, the boy,
wailing like a ghost in the wailing season.

Stop! begged Geppetto. But the boy
had set himself off like a car alarm
beneath the flight paths of magnetic geese.
Ah, my son, my son! God had Geppetto by the neck,
and was shaking him out

by the folds of his argument.
The fourth thing was lies, the fifth what lies
half-buried. Some damn thigh bone
of a bleached raggedy story. The sort of thing
that fathers whistle up, spitting in their palms

and knocking on wood.
The last thing, and the one after that,
was crookedness.
The difference between pain, and pain
without explanation. A limp creature

jerking between crossed sticks.
They were trying to quicken the almost-boy,
God in his lab coat and Geppetto in his wings.
But he kept getting tangled in the mesh
of cat flaps and cradles and strings.

WIFE OF SAINT CASAUBON OF THE LONG SILENCES AT THE BREAKFAST TABLE

To draw a halo use a pair of compasses.
When we lean together our burning profiles shatter
the black funerary urn between us.
Oh, nobody can work the negative spaces
like you, kiddo.

Embossing tools etch patterns onto gilt.
Then there is all that chewing to get through.
Tea? you ask suddenly, offering the teapot.
Sunlight cuts to the bone, the toast roars
flee not *tea*. *Blight, thunder, famine, blood.*

Angels spin like toys inside their whirling hours.
Your slow cistern-rage drains, drains, and fills up again,
as it does every winter morning.
And in the eastern sky an advertisement,
for the Constellation Mercy, clicks off.

Breakfast is the worst time for stigmata, the linens
a bloodbath. Thanks be Sister Hen for the bounty
of your eggs, Brother Frying Pan for your Teflon surface.
Kiddo, even the forks in their narrow kitchen drawers
dun themselves on your scribble-scribble flesh.

Tap lightly with hammer to preserve gold leaf.
Your hands loaded on the tablecloth. Fill.
And your spit-polished shoes, and the spaces between
your short ribs. Fill is what a marriage does, the opposite
of drip, empty, overflow, repeat.

Double the radius of grudging agreement
to measure fidelity, grievance, or the radiant ascent.
But I, I am lifted into that rigging of violence and air,
where the history of stars begins to shine.
And your halo buzzes like a cheap neon sign.

THE MARRIAGE SONNETS

I shall never forget the day I wrote The Mark on the Wall—*all in a flash, as if flying, after being kept stone breaking for months... and then Leonard came in, and I drank my milk, and concealed my excitement...*
— Virginia Woolf in a letter to Ethel Smyth, 16 October 1930

Leonard

First we buried you and then we dug you up again.
This was not the first time it had happened,
or even the second. The third time was a charm.
We thought you might stay dead, you
blue hieroglyph in the frozen earth. You bruise.
You you you, wearing your death skin so lightly
like a fur coat. The trees ran behind you, slipping
in the rain. They were playing a game called Statues.
Every time you looked back they froze into children
or the idea of children. They were not your children—
they were the mortal boys and unkissed girls
of life's longing for its other skin. Your knack,
lady, was for sufficiency. You never looked forward,
you never looked back.

Virginia

Begin in pain, in grit and strain. Salt.
Pearls irregular on the tongue,
we are. Pearls forlorn, pearls unworn,
we are. Our lustre dimmed, damned, dulled,
we die. Speak for yourself, oh string of pearls.
The swine before which I cast myself.
Little white stitches around the neck
hold me together. Some days arpeggio, they rise,
they rise. Hello, Gravity, why don't you put up your feet,
old stone. To rise above the house, snagging my sins.
Running along rooftops and hurling down chimney pots.
The children fly up in sparks, burn out, burn down
to ash. Then try, dead things, to crawl into my lap.
Pour me a glass of wine, dear Leonard, there's a chap.

Leonard

Oh stone breaker, you, down in your quarry
all morning. Your skin screeching like chalkboard
at the tip of a fingernail.
Each word breaks in two: all you do is tap it
with your terror.
Days pour themselves into wrong-shaped spaces,
but you put them to your lips, brave girl, and drink.
And every morning you smile your three smiles.
The first is snow needle, the second salt flinch,
the last what is left over
and over again. Grinning wears you thin,
all the pretty ones pressed inside their lockets.
But you, you wanted to be a real girl
with stones inside your pockets.

Virginia

Dip the comb in water, dear, then pull it through my hair.
Remember these are thoughts you're parting—brook
no imprecision there.
One day from the street you saw the hem of my dress
flying from the window, you saw the sun
shining through my lids. Those were pearls
that were my lies. *Pour me a glass of milk, dear.*
There's a chap. All day the hours fly up
like cinders from a cold fire.
Oh boulevardier! Standing there with the streets
snapping at your heels. Death and life
rattle about in me like a pair of dice
coming up Snake's Eyes or Devil's Cup
or Better Get Going, Girl, or Sorry, Time's Up.

Crooked

SHORT NOTE ON *HERE AM I*

What Abraham answers when God calls him to offer up his son, Isaac, as a burnt offering, and then again, what he replies when the Angel of the Lord calls out to absolve him of his sacrificial duty. *Here am I* (*Genesis* XXII).

Parents are always appalled by this story, children never are. They are used to being told what to do. Clean your room, go to bed. Lay your neck upon this altar. Shortly before the sacrificial moment, Isaac cries out to his father. Imagine a weary child calling in the mountainous night. This darkness lit only by conviction.

Abraham replies, *Here am I, my son.*

What could be more reassuring than this stalwart presentness? To God, to the angels, to a sleepy boy.

SHORT NOTE ON *THE PORTHOLE GAZE*

Vasco da Gama inflicted acts of great cruelty upon competing traders. The Portuguese historian, Gaspar Correia, describes what he calls The Pilgrim Ship Incident as one unequalled in cold-blooded cruelty. Da Gama looted a ship with over four hundred Muslim pilgrims on board; locking the passengers in the hold, he burnt them to death. Da Gama watched through the porthole while the women brought out their gold and jewels as ransom and held up their babies to beg for mercy. *Nada feito.*

In his *Gamíadas*, though, da Gama has a serene, declamatory tone as if he is calmed by the long aspect, the slight swell of the verse beneath his feet as he stands on deck. Looking on, looking out.

Is it possible that the Porthole Gaze, this minor act of staring intently, brought out the worst in the man? Or, as Correia would say, that having determined upon a course of great evil, da Gama could oversee its accomplishment only in tight close-up?

He liked to pretend that he was God, Correia wrote. But this was a fallacy because the Almighty does not crouch. He does not have to bend before the porthole of the world to watch our sufferings.

SHORT NOTE ON *MISTRANSLATION*

I've always loved the poem "Somnambule Ballad" by Federico García Lorca although, since Spanish is one of the thousands of languages in which I have no facility at all, I understand nothing of it. In the translation by Stephen Spender and J.L. Gili, the poets don't trouble to translate the title in its entirety as if there is no substitute for the word *somnambule*, at least not in English, that end-stopped, ungendered, slack-jawed version of a makeshift language.

Verde que te quiero verde, is the opening line of "*Romance Son Ambulo.*" It is mellifluous and beautiful and when one reads, it is difficult to keep one's hands from gesturing outwards, opening slightly to form the syllables. *Green, how much I want you green,* is the translated opening line of "Somnambule Ballad." A slightly comic line, it always makes me laugh with pleasure. And the disparity between the two lines—the one fluent and melodic, the other slightly willful like a cranky child tugging at one's sleeve—is the basis of my enduring fondness for this poem.

I believe this poem to be about the translation of the world into a colour so intense, so insistent, so demanding of the reader's passionate response, that everything is stained with it. Our hands where we have touched the page, and our eyes after we have read the last lines. Not a real colour, it is given a real colour's name so that we credulous readers might believe in it. We are, after all, *somnambulists!* Sleepwalkers in the lexicon of mistranslations.

SHORT NOTE ON *HUNGER*

Don't eat anything, dear. I'll come and get you as soon as I can, is what Demeter tells her daughter. But Persephone is hungry and snacks on a handful of pomegranate seeds, hence Winter.

Winter is what starves Hansel and Gretel's mama to the thigh bone of unreason. She leads her children into the wild forest because something wild is stalking her. Hunger turns a mother into a creature who ransoms her children to save herself. But Hansel and Gretel, natural foragers, find their own food in the forest and, one way or another, save themselves.

Persephone is both luckier and less lucky. Her mother forgives her for that momentary lapse into disobedience and junk food and travels barefoot into hell to save her daughter. She almost does too, the way mothers almost have for almost ever.

Hence post-Winter, a world in which daughters gnaw at themselves until blood wells to the surface. Such blood smells equally of cut flowers and the edge of the knife that cut them. It is called Hunger, it is called Spring.

SHORT NOTE ON *THANK YOU*

to the Manitoba Arts Council and the Winnipeg Arts Council for time.

to the editors of the following magazines for a place: *Arc Poetry Magazine, Cerise Press, Dusie* (Tuesday poem #56), *Literary Review of Canada, Prairie Fire, The Walrus.*

to mothers and daughters everywhere, "Easing the Spring" is for you (mine: Chana, Shoshana).

to the remarkable folks at Brick—the unsinkable Kitty McKay Lewis and my valiant editor, Barry Dempster, who put his finely-tuned ear to these monologues with eagerness and generosity. To Alayna Munce for her unblinking eye and intuitive touch. To David Seymour for blinking. To Natalie Waldburger for permission to use her extraordinary painting as my cover, and to Marijke Friesen, for turning it all upside down.

to the poets of this city for conversation. I'm talking to you Barb Schott, Charlene Diehl, Clarise Foster, Marjorie Poor.

to Mark Libin for buoyancy.

MÉIRA COOK has published three previous poetry collections with Brick Books. Her poetry has won first place in the CBC Literary Awards, and a poem from this collection won the inaugural Walrus Poetry Prize. Her first novel, *The House on Sugarbush Road*, won the McNally Robinson Manitoba Book of the Year Award. Her second novel, *Nightwatching*, will be published in May 2015. She lives, writes, and talks to herself in Winnipeg.